YOUR KNOWLEDGE HA

Bibliographic information published by the German National Library:

The German National Library lists this publication in the National Bibliography; detailed bibliographic data are available on the Internet at http://dnb.dnb.de .

Imprint:

Copyright © 2015 GRIN Verlag, Open Publishing GmbH
Print and binding: Books on Demand GmbH, Norderstedt Germany
ISBN: 978-3-668-05721-0

This book at GRIN:

http://www.grin.com/en/e-book/307331/analyzing-online-voting-systems-for-flaw-detection

Md. Shamsur Rahim, Ehtesham Chowdhury

Analyzing Online Voting Systems for Flaw Detection

GRIN Publishing

GRIN - Your knowledge has value

Since its foundation in 1998, GRIN has specialized in publishing academic texts by students, college teachers and other academics as e-book and printed book. The website www.grin.com is an ideal platform for presenting term papers, final papers, scientific essays, dissertations and specialist books.

Visit us on the internet:

http://www.grin.com/

http://www.facebook.com/grincom

http://www.twitter.com/grin_com

Analyzing Online Voting Systems for Flaw Detection

Md. Shamsur Rahim   **AZM Ehtesham Chowdhury**

Department of Computer Science

American International University- Bangladesh (AIUB), Dhaka,
Bangladesh

Abstract

Social media have already become a vital part in every aspects of our life because of the tre-
mendous advantage of technology. As a result, voting for contests are held online to provide
the users more comfort. Today people are voting for their favorite content or contestant in different types of contest via different forms of online voting policy. But regrettably the results of
these voting contests are not always reveal the actual result because of the manipulation of
voting using different tools and techniques. In this research paper, we have stated several case
studies concerning online voting manipulation. Case studies data are analyzed to discover how
computer technology is used to manipulate voting in Social Media for future research. The
study found that, there are many potential weaknesses that should be treated as highly hazardous
for online voting. We believe that, if these weaknesses can be resolved then online voting will
be more trustworthy as well widely acceptable. Even the possible solutions for the findings
from this paper can lead to elect representatives of parliament via Online Election System.

Keywords
Online Voting Contest, Online Election System, Social Media, Case Studies, Vote Manipulation.

Table of Contents

1. Introduction 3

2. Background Study 4

3. Case Studies 5

    3.1. Case 1: Photo Contest in Facebook 5

    3.2. Case 2: Voting through Tweets on Twitter using Hashtag 6

    3.3. Case 3: YouTube Video Contest 7

    3.4. Case 4: Product Review in E-Commerce Sites 8

    3.5. Case 5: Google Form's Poll Manipulation 9

4. Findings 12

5. Possible Characteristics of Futuristic Voting System 12

6. Conclusion 14

References 15

1. Introduction

In past few years technology has advanced so far away that digitization and automation has emerged on every aspects of human life, society and nation. Web technologies and networking have improved in a radical manner. Today different online contests are arranged by various companies. In this type of contests, online voting plays an important role. Different social media are providing different features (LIKE, hashtag, favorites). But in this types of contests, a big question has raised-"Is the system secured enough to held fail voting?" Because the voting result can be manipulated in various ways. Like in Facebook photo contests, number of fake accounts can be created or bought to give LIKES. And this will be unfair to the deserved candidate who can be the winner.

In online voting, it is very important to make a safe and secure environment to make the competition perfect and fair. For proper voting, a secure system is essential. In our research we have shown the flaws of online voting system in different social media, product review systems and voting forms. It is challenging job to make a system secured for online voting. There are some tradeoffs towards a secured system. For example, a system can be secured from bots [6] using high level captcha [1], but it will decrease user friendliness. And it leads to lessen popularity of that particular competition. There are no such effective solutions to detect fake IDs. The problems regarding online voting in not organized and explained so far. That leads our interest to study the cases to find out the reasons behind the security issue. As we know different developed and developing countries have started electronic voting on national election. Many countries do not start digitization on national election yet. But these types of manual voting are causing lots of manipulations on vote casting and riots occurred. With the emerging advantage of technology, now it's possible to arrange National Election via online. That can erase the manipulation. But there are flaws in online voting system. So, national election cannot be arranged online so far. Before this, a secure online voting system essential. Our motivation behind this research was to find out the flaws behind online competition. In this paper we have discussed **five** cases and found the reasons behind the unfair competitions on online. As, digitalization is evolved on every aspects, security is the burning issue here. As elections have to be fair and proper leader must have to win for the welfare for the nation and society, online election also have to be more secure than manual voting. Our focus on this paper is to mark the problems and flaws on online security for fair voting that have to be eradicated. That will lead to national and local elections online.

2. Background Study

Online Contest: Different types of online contests are arranged in different social media. Users are select a content or topic by giving Like (Facebook), Favorites (Twitter, YouTube). It is actually process of proving content popular among other contents. Different photo contests, best couple contests, best songs, video contests and writing contests are arranged by different social media.

Like: It is a way to give positive feedback on contents and connect with things a particular user or user group care about. Users can "like" content such as status updates, comments, photos, and links posted by friends, pages, groups, and advertisers [2]. The number of likes that posts receive is one factor that Facebook uses to determine what to show in News Feed.

Subscribe: The feature allows users to follow public updates, and these are the people most often broadcasting their ideas [3]. The main purpose of this feature is to keep the fan page and continue to maintain two separate Facebook presences.

Contest Apps: Facebook has an application feature which is used to start a Timeline or Page Contest. There are many types of contests like photo contest, app concepts, and idea contests. Here different users give their vote to contestants by the "like" feature.

Hash Tag Feature: Online user judging or voting is also sometimes arranged by using feature like "hashtag". The main difference lies between features using "like" and "timeline" [4]. The positive or supportive feedback is given using #hashtag [5] on timeline.

Tweets: In Twitter "tweet" is some sort of messages or microblog text that express the thoughts, idea, and interests on some issue or content. Default feature is that tweets are visible publicly, but senders can restrict message delivery to just their followers [26]. Retweeting is when a tweet is forwarded via Twitter by users. It is actually same as share in "Facebook". Both tweets and retweets can be tracked to see which ones are most popular. #Hashtag tweets are one of the best ways for voting in online contests. A celebrity or a person how much popular can be get by twitter hashtag and follower as it is a microblog.

Fake Accounts: Fake means anything that doesn't belongs to actual thing. In social media fake account is the account which is not belongs to the actual person. Information of a particular person is manipulated or faked by another person. In different mailboxes (Gmail, Yahoo Mail), social networking sites (Facebook, Twitter) and video sharing sites (YouTube), fake accounts can be created. These fake accounts are used in different unethical and unfair purposes. By using these accounts anyone can harm a user and make a contest unfair.

Internet Bot: An Internet bot, in its most generic sense, is software that performs an automated task over the Internet. More specifically, a bot is an automated application used to perform simple and repetitive tasks that would be time-consuming, mundane or impossible for a human to perform [6]. Bots can be used for productive tasks, but they are also frequently used for malicious purposes. The term "bot" comes from robot. An Internet bot may also be known as a Web robot or WWW robot. Website scrapers that grab the content of websites and re-use it without permission on automatically generated doorway pages [6]. One of the best examples of a good bot is a search engine spider. Such bots troll the Web and index new pages for a search engine. Other examples include the original Internet relay chat bots and chatterbots. A feed bot is a type of Internet Bot that scrapes content in part or in full from either RSS feeds or whole Unified Resource Locator (URL) links as their source of content.

3. Case Studies

Here in this section, we mention several case studies related to online voting manipulation on Social media.

3.1. Case 1: Photo Contest in Facebook

Facebook is the largest online social network with total 1,310,000,000 monthly active Facebook users [7]. Because of this reason, Facebook is one of the tempting choice to the Companies for branding purpose. Companies host different types of campaign in Facebook with the intention of reaching and recruiting new fans, launching new products and services, building email sub-scriber list, increasing awareness and staying top of mind etc. [8]. Photo Contest Campaign is one of the attractive option among many options for branding purpose.

Join Banglalink Opera Photo Contest & win PLAY W17 SMARTPHONE, the coolest smartphone in the town, every day.

All you have to do is, download Opera Mini browser, upload your photo using "UPLOAD PHOTO & WIN PLAY W17 SMARTPHONE" speed dial & share your photo on Facebook & twitter.

The photo with the most number of likes will win PLAY W17 SMARTPHONE every day. Join the contest now!

To download opera mini browser please visit http://m.opera.com

Like · Comment · Share

Figure 1: Sample Photo Contest on Facebook [9]

In most of the Photo Contests, users are required to upload their best photo regarding a special occasion and get as much as "Like" possible from the users. Although it's a good promotional method for the Promoters, but in most of cases well-deserved contestants are being deprived because of vote manipulation. At present, there are many sources [10, 11] highly available on the internet from where anyone can buy their desired "Likes" even Verified Facebook Accounts [12, 13]. In case of purchased Facebook accounts, it's possible to cast vote through BOT by using these purchased accounts.

3.2. Case 2: Voting through Tweets on Twitter using Hashtag

Twitter is the second largest online social network with 289,000,000 users in terms of active users [14]. Tweets of Twitter is a good choice to the different organizations for promotional purposes as they can their photos, videos, updates etc. [15]. Using the "hashtag" feature of Twitter, many voting contests are hosted by different organizations. For example, America's Got Talent (@nbcagt) had Twitter voting on their show.

Figure 2: Sample Tweet for Voting [16]

Again, this type of voting can be easily manipulated using automated vote casting software. The voting result from the social networks like Twitter also have influence over the result of National Election [17] so it's essential to stop voting manipulation to make it more reliable.

3.3. Case 3: YouTube Video Contest

In YouTube there are many channels associated with a google account where user can subscribe the channels. Different companies marketing their product or content through different type of video contests. In figure 3 we can see the contest named "Best ICC T20 Cricket World Cup 2014 Flash MOB". In this contest different educational institutions of Bangladesh have made videos of own flash mob of the theme song of T20 Cricket World Cup. So the winner is selected by counting number of views [18]. Here view number can be increased. This approach is done by using a script that can be automated to reload the same link of the video in a browser. So the number views will be increased automatically. So "How can it be a fair contest?"

Figure 3: Most Popular ICC T20 World Cup Theme Song Flash Mob [19]

3.4. Case 4: Product Review in E-Commerce Sites

Ecommerce sites have made product procuring easier than anything before. According to [20], B2C e-commerce sales are expected to reach 1.92 trillion U.S. dollars worldwide by 2016.

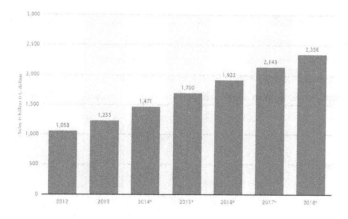

Figure 4: B2C E-commerce sales Worldwide [20]

8

In this gigantic market, people mostly buy their essential products by viewing the feedbacks/ reviews from the other customers about the product/ supplier. But this kind of reviews/feedbacks can be easily tampered by writing fake reviews through man power/ automation tools.

This type of tampering feedbacks/ reviews causes the buyers heavy financial loss and also damage the reputation of that site [22]. By ensuring real feedbacks, growth rate and popularity can be boosted highly.

Figure 5: Sample Review [21]

3.5. Case 5: Google Form's Poll Manipulation

Because of the user friendly feature, Google form [23] is an excellent way to collect survey or poll result vastly around the World. Sometimes, voting for different contest are held with the help of Google Form. With the help of Software Bot, it's possible to cast thousands of votes just in an hour. Although, in Google Form "one vote per person" restriction can be implied by mandating login, but the security of Google form is not enough to prevent voting manipulation. For an experiment, we have created a Google Form. In that form, users are required to answer a question and submit it with their Name.

Online Vote Manipulation

* Required

Do you think that, Online Voting Result can be manipulated? *

- ○ Strongly Agree
- ○ Agree
- ○ Disagree
- ○ Strongly Disagree

Your Name: *

[   ]

[Submit]

Never submit passwords through Google Forms.

Powered by
Google Forms

This content is neither created nor endorsed by Google.
Report Abuse - Terms of Service - Additional Terms

Figure 6: Sample Form for experiment purpose [24]

In the next step, we have implemented a script using Selenium [25] that can cast vote with fake names and desired answer. To develop a reliable polling system, a system should detect multiple vote casting.

Table 1: Sample Code Snippet for submitting a Google Form automatically

```
static void Main(string[] args)
{
int count = 0;
driver = new FirefoxDriver();
string baseURL =
"https://docs.google.com/forms/d/1SUHyAUKJahLKrNENUNw1MI1RnVgfzy_5jE_vO8ci3sA/viewform";

string[] lines = System.IO.File.ReadAllLines(@"C:\com.txt");
List<string> names = new List<string>();
foreach (string line in lines)
  names.Add(line);

for (int i = 0; i < names.Count; i++)
{
  VotingMethod(driver, names[i]);
  Console.Write(". " + count);
  Thread.Sleep(1000);
}

Console.WriteLine("Press any key to exit.");
System.Console.ReadKey();
}

public static void VotingMethod(IWebDriver driver, string Name)
{
driver.Navigate().GoToUrl(baseURL);
driver.FindElement(By.Id("group_235897043_1")).Click();
driver.FindElement(By.Id("entry_185653720")).Clear();
driver.FindElement(By.Id("entry_185653720")).SendKeys(Name);
driver.FindElement(By.Id("ss-submit")).Click();
}
```

4. Findings

1. Case 3 shows a video contest can be won by manipulating the number of views. In this case, we have taken the most popular video sharing site, YouTube in our consideration. Simply a script can increase the number of views automatically in a shorter time by refreshing the same link. To arrange this kind of video contest, a system should be able to identify unique viewer.

2. Case 1 & 2 depicts that in Facebook photo contest and Twitter #hashtag enabled contests are being manipulated by fake accounts. Few people buy the fake accounts, give like from those accounts. There is not such a way to stop fake accounts or bot from giving likes or tweeting posts.

3. In Case 4, we have shown that product review can be manipulated by fake accounts. Without some top e-commerce sites, other sites don't have any security approach to stop from giving fake review. So different companies pay money to others to give positive review for the products.

4. No efficient algorithm/ framework for detecting the fake accounts and user.

5. No effective approach to prevent a bot from manipulation.

6. Different types of social media, require different types of voting models.

5. Possible Characteristics of Futuristic Voting System

Analysis shows that online voting can be manipulated on many ways. Using of BOTs for rapid voting is popular weapon. If a BOT frequently hit on voting website using multiple user accounts then it is possible to alter the actual winner as discussed on the section 4. It can be stopped by implementing some mechanisms on that site.

1. Detection of user IP address and device number or MAC address for keeping track of the particular device used for voting. Every time system will check for particular device that is used for voting or not. For a personal computer or mobile vote should be given by one user. Usually it is not normal to multiple voting submission from one device.

2. In case of online voting contests through YouTube or other social networking sites multiple view or voting is permitted. On this type of system using of BOT can be prevented by using a captcha. The captcha question can be related to the particular content of voting or related to the user itself or other current issues. A simple intelligent BOT also cannot answer the questions. **NLPs** [27] and **Intelligent Image Processing** [28] cannot be done by the BOT.

3. Sometimes voters will give their votes from cybercafé. For that characteristic 2 will be helpful. In that case captcha will appear after submitting vote. If captcha is appeared on opening of the page it will be disturbing and demoralize to vote.

4. An algorithm can be designed to make the IP address and MAC address unique combination. As we know MAC is unique like IMEI of mobile. But a single IP can be used on different cluster of internet on different location as IPV4 addresses are limited.

5. Another solution can be IPV6. IPV6 contains the interface address. The NIC card or MAC address. IPV6 address is unique unlike IPV4. The transition to IPv6 is inevitable, but migration requires considerable effort, preparation and consideration [29].

Above we have mentioned possible solutions can be used for futuristic voting systems for fair voting. Intelligent Biometric recognition systems through secure connection can lead to fair and efficient online National Election System.

6. Conclusion

Currently online voting is not widely manipulated and people are participating spontaneously. But day by day people are getting familiar with online voting manipulation and they are taking their face off from these types of voting system. It's high time to stop online voting manipulation to hold the spontaneous participation keep going. Our findings suggest that, different types of social media require different types of security models for vote casting. Hence online voting manipulation can be avoided and it can lead us to arrange National Election via online. Our findings also suggest that, we shouldn't trade off security issue with user friendly system. Rather we should focus on both.

References

[1] CAPTCHA, See at: https://en.wikipedia.org/wiki/CAPTCHA

[2] Like, See at: https://www.facebook.com/help/452446998120360

[3] Subscription, See at: http://mashable.com/2011/09/15/facebook-subscribe-users/

[4] Timeline, See at: http://www.romcartridge.com/2011/12/what-is-facebook-timeline.html

[5] Hashtag, See at: http://www.techstake.org/2013/06/facebook-introduces-hashtags-to-its-users.html

[6] Internet Bot, See at: http://www.techopedia.com/definition/24063/internet-bot

[7] Facebook Active User Statistics, See at: http://www.statisticbrain.com/facebook-statistics/

[8] Best Facebook Contests, See at: http://www.agorapulse.com/blog/best-facebook-contests-2014

[9] Opera Photo Contest on Facebook, See at: https://www.facebook.com/bangla-linkmela/posts/771906909519936

[10] Get Your Likes, See at: http://www.getyourlikes.co.uk/

[11] Boost Likes, See at: https://boostlikes.com/

[12] Verified Facebook Account, See at: https://www.facebook.com/help/196050490547892

[13] Verified Facebook Accounts Purchase, See at: http://facebookpvastore.com/

[14] Tweeter active user statistics, See at: http://www.statisticbrain.com/twitter-statistics/

[15] Burton, Suzan, and Alena Soboleva. "Interactive or reactive? Marketing with Twitter." Journal of Consumer Marketing 28.7 (2011): 491-499.

[16] Twitter Voting, See at: https://media.twitter.com/best-practice/twitter-voting

[17] Metaxas, Takis, and Eni Mustafaraj. "Social media and the elections." (2012)

[18] Result of Contest hosted in YouTube, See at: http://en.wikipedia.org/wiki/Char_Chokka_Hoi_Hoi

[19] Most Popular ICC T20 World Cup Theme Song Flash Mob, https://www.youtube.com/playlist?list=PLtWkiFWAD1cyz8ayhBgjVUoC_paC_pRE4

[20] B2C E-Commerce Sales Amount, See at: http://www.statista.com/statistics/261245/b2c-e-commerce-sales-worldwide/

[21] Review for Product, See at: http://www.flipkart.com/lenovo-flex-2-14d-notebook-apu-quad-core-a6-4gb-500gb-8gb-ssd-win8-1-59-427873/p/itmdxea6mwz3chkc?pid=COMDXEA3AZSECZKT&ref=L%3A-8240404855483645232&srno=b_1

[22] Corbitt, Brian J., Theerasak Thanasankit, and Han Yi. "Trust and e-commerce: a study of consumer perceptions." Electronic commerce research and applications 2.3 (2003): 203-215

[23] Google Form, See at: https://www.google.com/forms/about/

[24] Sample Google Form, See at: https://docs.google.com/forms/d/1SU-HyAUKJahLKrNENUN w1Mi1RnVgfzy_5jE_vO8ci3sA/viewform

[25] Holmes, Antawan, and Marc Kellogg. "Automating functional tests using selenium." Agile Conference, 2006. IEEE, 2006

[26] Twitter tweet feature, see at: http://en.wikipedia.org/wiki/Twitter

[27] Collobert, Ronan, and Jason Weston. "A unified architecture for natural language processing: Deep neural networks with multitask learning."Proceedings of the 25th international conference on Machine learning. ACM, 2008.

[28] Nixon, Mark. Feature extraction & image processing. Academic Press, 2008.

[29] Wikipedia contributors. IPv6 address. Wikipedia, The Free Encyclopedia. June 3, 2015, 00:30 UTC. Available at: http://en.wikipedia.org/w/index.php?title=IPv6_address&oldid=665255110. Accessed June 5, 2015.

YOUR KNOWLEDGE HAS VALUE

- We will publish your bachelor's and master's thesis, essays and papers

- Your own eBook and book - sold worldwide in all relevant shops

- Earn money with each sale

Upload your text at www.GRIN.com
and publish for free